Sizzlin

WOK

Your Promise of Success

Welcome to the world of Confident Cooking, created for you in our
test kitchen, where recipes are double-tested by our team of home
economists to achieve a high standard of success.

PERIPLUS

Wielding a wok

We all have our favourite culinary utensils, but few are as versatile as the wok. A wok is the ultimate tool for healthy, tasty stir-fries, as well as deep-frying, steaming and even smoking foods.

Preparing meals in a wok requires a little organisation and preparation, but the cooking time itself is minimal due to the high heat and large surface area of a wok.

There are several different types of wok on the market: traditional rolled steel; cast iron; stainless steel; aluminium; non-stick; and electric. The type of wok you use is your choice, but the traditional rolled steel and cast iron woks are the best heat conductors and will promote better searing and flavour, especially when used on a gas stove top.

A traditional rolled steel wok.

Non-stick woks are easy to clean and need little oil for cooking, making them an even healthier option.

Electric woks are convenient, but make sure you buy one with the highest wattage possible, otherwise it may not get hot enough.

Buy an electric wok with a high wattage.

Utensils needed to cook with a wok are minimal. There is only one tool which is a necessity—a wok turner or *charn*—a spade-like scoop ideal for the continuous, fast scooping and turning required when stir-frying. Always use a plastic charn when cooking in a non-stick wok—if you scratch it

Mesh ladles, a charn and some chopsticks.

you will ruin the non-stick surface.

If you are deep-frying in a wok, a mesh ladle is good for lifting and draining the fried food. A pair of long wooden chopsticks are also useful when deep-frying to turn things over so they brown and crisp evenly.

SEASONING
YOUR WOK
Seasoning a wok starts the process of *wok hay* development. Wok hay is a filmy layer of residue that cooks onto the wok with the high cooking heat and, with time, becomes a brownish black colour. It imparts the distinctive Asian

flavour and gives a nice smooth surface which helps prevent the food from sticking. It is not harmful and should never be scrubbed off.

Rolled steel woks are usually coated with a thin lacquer to prevent rusting before being sold and this must be removed before seasoning. To do this, place the wok on the stove top, fill it with cold water and add 2 tablespoons of bicarbonate of soda. Bring the water to the boil and boil rapidly for 15 minutes. Drain and scrub off the lacquer with a scourer, repeating the process if there is any lacquer remaining. Rinse and dry the wok thoroughly. Have a small bowl of peanut or corn oil and paper towels ready.

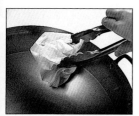

Dip the towels in the oil and wipe over the wok.

Place the wok over high heat, then scrunch up a handful of paper towels, dip the towels in the oil and wipe over the entire inner surface of the wok—you may wish to use some long-handled tongs. Repeat until the paper towels come away clean from the wok. Then turn the heat to low and leave for 15 minutes so the wok can absorb the oil. Repeat just prior to using your wok for the first time.

CARING FOR
YOUR WOK
A properly seasoned wok or a non-stick wok should rarely if ever be scoured on the inside with an abrasive material like steel wool. The outside, however, may occasionally need a good going over. Try not to use detergents unless necessary—they damage the seasoning. If you do burn something, you may need to use detergent and even a fine steel wool to clean your wok. However, your wok will need to be re-seasoned.

When you have finished cooking and your wok has cooled down, wash it with hot water and a soft brush or cloth. Make sure you dry it thoroughly before storing in a dry area. If you have a steel wok you should wipe or brush the inside with a very thin layer of oil before putting it away—this will keep it in tiptop condition.

TIPS FOR
SUCCESSFUL
STIR-FRYING
● Stir-fry meat in batches to prevent too much liquid being released, causing the meat to stew and toughen.

Stir-fry meat in batches to avoid stewing.

● Prepare all the ingredients before you start to ensure quick and even cooking.

Prepare all the ingredients before you start to cook.

● Do not cover the wok during cooking or the food will steam.
● Turn the food continuously to ensure even cooking.

Sizzling Wok

Using a wok is no longer an exotic, 'foreign' method of cooking. Indeed, cooking with a wok is easy, delicious and healthy.

Asian peppered beef

Preparation time:
  10 minutes +
  2 hours marinating
Total cooking time:
  12 minutes
Serves 4

600 g beef (skirt steak), thinly sliced
2 cloves garlic, finely chopped
2 teaspoons finely chopped fresh ginger
2 onions, thinly sliced
2 tablespoons Chinese rice wine
1 teaspoon sesame oil
1 tablespoon soy sauce
1 tablespoon oyster sauce
2 teaspoons sugar
1 teaspoon Sichuan peppercorns, crushed
1 tablespoon black peppercorns, crushed
2 spring onions, chopped into 2.5 cm lengths
2 tablespoons oil

1. Place the beef strips in a large bowl. Add the garlic, ginger, onion, rice wine, sesame oil, soy sauce, oyster sauce, sugar and peppercorns, and mix together well. Cover and marinate in the refrigerator for at least 2 hours.
2. Drain, discarding any excess liquid, and stir in the spring onion.
3. Heat a wok until very hot, add half the oil and swirl to coat. Add half the beef and stir-fry for 6 minutes, or until seared and cooked to your liking. Repeat with the remaining oil and beef. Serve with boiled rice.

NUTRITION PER SERVE
Protein 40 g; Fat 15 g; Carbohydrate 6 g; Dietary Fibre 1 g; Cholesterol 117 mg; 1400 kJ (335 cal)

Note: The wok needs to be searing hot for this recipe. The beef is easier to slice if it is partially frozen.

Asian peppered beef

Singapore noodles

Preparation time:
  20 minutes +
  30 minutes soaking +
  30 minutes marinating
Total cooking time:
  10 minutes
Serves 4–6

400 g dried rice
  vermicelli
2 cloves garlic, crushed
2 teaspoons grated
  fresh ginger
1/4 cup (60 ml) oyster
  sauce
1/4 cup (60 ml) soy sauce
250 g chicken breast
  fillets, thinly sliced
2 tablespoons oil
2 sticks celery, julienned
1 large carrot, julienned
3 spring onions, sliced
  on the diagonal
1 1/2 tablespoons Asian
  curry powder
1/2 teaspoon sesame oil
65 g bean sprouts

1. Cover the noodles with cold water and leave for 30 minutes, or until soft. Drain.
2. Place the garlic, ginger, 1 tablespoon oyster sauce and 2 teaspoons soy sauce in a bowl and mix well. Add the chicken, toss to coat and marinate for 30 minutes.

3. Heat a wok until very hot, add the oil and swirl to coat. Stir-fry the chicken until browned. Add the celery, carrot and half the spring onion, and stir-fry for 2–3 minutes, or until slightly softened. Add the curry powder and stir-fry for 2 minutes, or until aromatic.
4. Add the noodles and mix well to coat and heat through. Then stir in the remaining oyster sauce, soy sauce, spring onion, sesame oil and bean sprouts. Serve hot.

NUTRITION PER SERVE (6)
Protein 13 g; Fat 12 g; Carbohydrate 20 g; Dietary Fibre 2.5 g; Cholesterol 20 mg; 1003 kJ (240 cal)

Chilli beef with cashews

Preparation time:
  10 minutes
Total cooking time:
  12 minutes
Serves 4–6

1/4 cup (60 ml) peanut
  oil
600 g rump steak,
  thinly sliced
1 onion, cut into wedges
2 cloves garlic, crushed
1/4 cup (60 ml) beef
  stock
2 tablespoons soy
  sauce
1 tablespoon oyster
  sauce
1 tablespoon chilli bean
  sauce
2 teaspoons cornflour
1 red capsicum,
  julienned
200 g snow peas
1/2 cup (80 g) cashews,
  toasted

1. Heat a wok until very hot, add 1 tablespoon oil and swirl to coat. Add half the beef and stir-fry for 4 minutes, or until browned. Repeat with another tablespoon oil and the remaining beef. Remove.
2. Add the remaining oil to the wok and swirl to coat. Add the onion and stir-fry for 1 minute. Add the garlic and stir-fry for another minute.
3. Place the stock, soy, oyster and chilli bean sauces and cornflour in a bowl, mix well and add to the wok. Add the capsicum and snow peas. Return the beef to the wok and stir-fry for 2 minutes, or until the vegetables are just cooked but still crunchy. Stir in the cashews and serve with boiled rice.

NUTRITION PER SERVE (6)
Protein 29 g; Fat 19 g; Carbohydrate 8.5 g; Dietary Fibre 3.5 g; Cholesterol 65 mg; 1325 kJ (317 cal)

Singapore noodles (top) and Chilli beef with cashews

Tempura

Preparation time:
  20 minutes
Total cooking time:
  15 minutes
Serves 4–6

12 raw king prawns,
  peeled, deveined,
  tails intact
oil, for deep-frying
1¹/4 cups (200 g)
  tempura flour
1 egg yolk
1 small red capsicum,
  sliced
150 g orange sweet
  potato, thinly sliced
100 g broccoli florets
soy sauce, to serve

1. Slice the prawns
lengthways, without
cutting all the way
through, to butterfly.
2. Fill a wok one third
full of oil and heat until
a cube of bread dropped
into the oil browns in
15 seconds. Place the
flour in a bowl, add
the egg yolk and 1 cup
(250 ml) iced water
and stir gently with
chopsticks until just
combined and slightly
lumpy.
3. Dip each prawn in
the batter, up to the tail,
and cook in batches
for 2–3 minutes, or until
lightly golden. Drain.
4. Dip the vegetables in
the batter and cook in
batches until lightly
golden. Drain. Serve
with soy sauce.

NUTRITION PER SERVE (6)
Protein 13 g; Fat 7.8 g;
Carbohydrate 30 g; Dietary
Fibre 2.5 g; Cholesterol
85 mg; 1001 kJ (240 cal)

Pad Thai noodles

Preparation time:
  30 minutes +
  10 minutes soaking
Total cooking time:
  7 minutes
Serves 4–6

250 g thick rice stick
  noodles
1 red chilli, chopped
2 cloves garlic, chopped
2 spring onions,
  chopped
1¹/2 tablespoons sugar
2 tablespoons fish sauce
2 tablespoons lime juice
1 tablespoon tamarind
  purée, combined with
  1 tablespoon water
2 tablespoons oil
2 eggs, beaten
150 g pork fillet, thinly
  sliced
8 raw large prawns,
  peeled, deveined,
  tails intact
100 g fried tofu,
  julienned
1 cup (90 g) bean sprouts
¹/4 cup (7 g) fresh
  coriander leaves
¹/4 cup (40 g) chopped
  roasted peanuts
1 lime, cut into wedges

1. Cover the noodles
with water and soak
for 10 minutes. Drain.
2. Using a mortar and
pestle, or blender, pound
the chilli, garlic and
spring onion, gradually
incorporating the sugar,
fish sauce, lime juice
and tamarind mixture.
3. Heat a wok until very
hot, add 1 tablespoon
of the oil and swirl to
coat. Add the egg, swirl
to coat and cook for
1–2 minutes, or until
set and cooked through.
Remove and shred.
4. Heat the remaining
oil, add the chilli
mixture, and stir-fry for
30 seconds, or until
fragrant. Add the pork
and stir-fry for 2 minutes,
or until just tender. Add
the prawns and stir-fry
for 1 minute.
5. Add the noodles,
egg, tofu and half the
bean sprouts, and toss
to heat through.
6. Serve immediately
topped with remaining
bean sprouts, coriander,
peanuts and lime.

NUTRITION PER SERVE (6)
Protein 18 g; Fat 14 g;
Carbohydrate 17 g; Dietary
Fibre 2.5 g; Cholesterol
110 mg; 1126 kJ (270 cal)

Tempura (top)
and Pad Thai noodles

Pumpkin and coconut curry

Preparation time:
 20 minutes
Total cooking time:
 30 minutes
Serves 4

2 tablespoons sesame
 seeds
1 tablespoon peanut oil
1 brown onion, finely
 chopped
3 cloves garlic, crushed
2 teaspoons finely
 chopped fresh ginger
1 teaspoon ground
 coriander
2 teaspoons ground
 cumin
2 teaspoons finely
 chopped red chilli
800 g pumpkin, cut
 into 2 cm cubes
1 cup (250 ml) coconut
 cream
1 cup (250 ml)
 vegetable stock
2 tablespoons fresh
 coriander leaves

1. Heat a wok until very
hot. Add the sesame
seeds and stir-fry for
1–2 minutes, or until
toasted. Remove.
Add the oil and swirl
to coat. Add the
onion and stir-fry for
3 minutes, or until soft
and golden. Add the
garlic, ginger, spices
and chilli, and stir-fry
for 1 minute, or until
fragrant.
2. Add the pumpkin,
stir-fry for 1 minute,
then pour in the
coconut cream and
stock and bring to the
boil. Reduce the heat
and simmer, loosely
covered, for 10 minutes.
Uncover and simmer
for 5–10 minutes, or
until the pumpkin is
tender and the liquid has
reduced and thickened.
3. Season with salt and
scatter with the sesame
seeds and coriander.

NUTRITION PER SERVE
*Protein 8 g; Fat 25 g;
Carbohydrate 17 g; Dietary
Fibre 5 g; Cholesterol 0 mg;
1263 kJ (300 cal)*

San choy bau

Preparation time:
 30 minutes +
 20 minutes soaking
Total cooking time:
 12 minutes
Serves 4

2 dried Chinese
 mushrooms
2 tablespoons oil
200 g pork mince
100 g chicken mince
2 cloves garlic, crushed
3 cm fresh ginger, grated
1 stick celery, finely
 chopped
50 g green beans, sliced
1/4 red capsicum, finely
 chopped
1/3 cup (50 g) water
 chestnuts, chopped
2 teaspoons Golden
 Mountain sauce
2 tablespoons oyster
 sauce
1 tablespoon soy sauce
1/4 teaspoon sugar
1 iceberg lettuce

1. Cover the mushrooms
with hot water and
leave for 20 minutes.
Drain, discard the
stems and finely chop.
2. Heat a wok until very
hot, add half the oil
and swirl to coat. Add
the pork, chicken,
garlic and ginger, and
stir-fry for 5 minutes,
or until the meat
changes colour. Break
up any lumps. Add the
celery, beans and
capsicum, and stir-fry
for 3 minutes. Add the
water chestnuts, Golden
Mountain, oyster and
soy sauces and sugar.
Stir-fry for 1 minute.
3. Trim each lettuce leaf
into a cup and place
1–2 heaped tablespoons
of the filling into each
cup. Roll up and eat
with your fingers.

NUTRITION PER SERVE
*Protein 20 g; Fat 11 g;
Carbohydrate 6 g; Dietary
Fibre 2 g; Cholesterol
37 mg; 838 kJ (200 cal)*

*Pumpkin and coconut curry (top)
and San choy bau*

Mee Grob

Preparation time:
35 minutes +
20 minutes soaking
Total cooking time:
15 minutes
Serves 4–6

4 dried Chinese
  mushrooms
oil, for deep-frying
100 g dried rice vermicelli
100 g fried tofu, cut
  into matchsticks
4 cloves garlic, crushed
1 onion, chopped
200 g pork fillet, thinly
  sliced
1 chicken breast fillet,
  thinly sliced
8 green beans, sliced on
  the diagonal
6 spring onions, thinly
  sliced on the diagonal
8 raw prawns, peeled,
  deveined
30 g bean sprouts
fresh coriander leaves,
  to garnish

Sauce
1 tablespoon soy sauce
3 tablespoons white
  vinegar
3 tablespoons sugar
3 tablespoons fish sauce
1 tablespoon chilli sauce

1. Cover the mushrooms
with hot water and
soak for 20 minutes.
Drain, discard the
stems and thinly slice.
2. Fill a wok one third
full of oil and heat until
a cube of bread browns
in 15 seconds. Cook
the noodles in batches
for 20 seconds, or until
puffed and crispy.
Drain and cool.
3. Add the tofu to the
wok in batches and
cook for 1 minute,
or until crisp. Drain.
Carefully ladle out
all but 2 tablespoons
of the oil.
4. Reheat the wok until
very hot. Add the garlic
and onion, and stir-fry
for 1 minute. Add
the pork and stir-fry for
3 minutes. Add the
chicken, beans,
mushrooms and half
the spring onion, and
stir-fry for 2 minutes,
or until the chicken has
almost cooked through.
Add the prawns and
stir-fry for 2 minutes,
or until just tender.
5. Combine the sauce
ingredients in a bowl,
add to the wok and
stir-fry for 2 minutes,
or until the meat and
prawns are tender.
6. Remove from the
heat and stir in the
bean sprouts, tofu and
noodles. Garnish with
the coriander and the
remaining spring onion.

NUTRITION PER SERVE (6)
*Protein 25 g; Fat 10 g;
Carbohydrate 17 g; Dietary
Fibre 2.5 g; Cholesterol
72 mg; 1055 kJ (255 cal)*

Mee Grob

*Slice down the back of the prawns and
remove the intestinal tract.*

*Cook the rice vermicelli noodles until
they are puffed and crispy.*

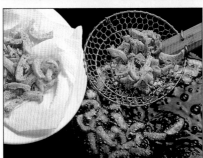

Add the tofu to the wok in batches and cook until crisp.

Stir-fry for 2 minutes, or until the prawns are just tender.

13

Many mushroom noodles

Preparation time:
  30 minutes +
  20 minutes soaking
Total cooking time:
  15 minutes
Serves 4–6

25 g dried Chinese
  mushrooms
1 tablespoon oil
¹/2 teaspoon sesame oil
1 tablespoon finely
  chopped fresh ginger
4 cloves garlic, crushed
100 g fresh shiitake
  mushrooms, trimmed,
  sliced
150 g oyster
  mushrooms, sliced
150 g shimeji
  mushrooms, trimmed,
  pulled apart
³/4 cup (185 ml) dashi
  (see Note)
¹/4 cup (60 ml) soy
  sauce
¹/4 cup (60 ml) mirin
25 g butter
2 tablespoons lemon
  juice
100 g enoki mushrooms,
  trimmed, pulled apart
500 g thin Hokkien
  noodles, separated
1 tablespoon chopped
  fresh chives

1. Soak the Chinese mushrooms in 1¹/2 cups (375 ml) boiling water for 20 minutes, or until soft. Drain, reserving the liquid. Discard the stems and slice the caps.
2. Heat a wok until very hot, add the oils and swirl to coat. Add the ginger, garlic, shiitake, oyster and shimeji mushrooms, and stir-fry for 1–2 minutes, or until the mushrooms have wilted. Remove.
3. Combine the dashi, soy, mirin, ¹/4 teaspoon white pepper and ³/4 cup (185 ml) reserved liquid, add to the wok and cook for 3 minutes. Add the butter, lemon juice and 1 teaspoon salt and cook for 1 minute, or until the sauce thickens. Return the mushrooms to the wok, cook for 2 minutes, then stir in the enoki and Chinese mushrooms.
4. Add the noodles and stir for 3 minutes, or until heated through. Sprinkle with the chives and serve immediately.

NUTRITION PER SERVE (6)
Protein 15 g; Fat 8.5 g; Carbohydrate 60 g; Dietary Fibre 5 g; Cholesterol 25 mg; 1610 kJ (385 cal)

Note: To make the dashi, dissolve 1¹/2 teaspoons dashi powder in ³/4 cup (185 ml) water.

Braised bok choy

Preparation time:
  10 minutes
Total cooking time:
  5 minutes
Serves 4 (as a side dish)

2 tablespoons peanut
  oil
1 clove garlic, crushed
1 tablespoon shredded
  fresh ginger
550 g bok choy,
  separated, cut into
  8 cm lengths
1 teaspoon sugar
1 teaspoon sesame oil
1 tablespoon oyster
  sauce

1. Heat a wok until very hot, add the oil and swirl to coat. Add the garlic and ginger, and stir-fry for 1–2 minutes, then add the bok choy and stir-fry for 1 minute. Add the sugar, a pinch of salt, cracked black pepper and ¹/4 cup (60 ml) water. Bring to the boil, then reduce the heat and simmer, covered, for 3 minutes, or until the stems are tender but crisp.
2. Stir in the sesame oil and oyster sauce and serve immediately.

NUTRITION PER SERVE
Protein 7 g; Fat 11 g; Carbohydrate 3 g; Dietary Fibre 6 g; Cholesterol 0 mg; 582 kJ (139 cal)

*Many mushroom noodles (top)
and Braised bok choy*

Whole steamed fish

Preparation time:
  30 minutes
Total cooking time:
  25 minutes
Serves 4

1 (900 g) whole
  snapper, cleaned
  and scaled
10 small sprigs fresh
  coriander
1 lime, thinly sliced
10 cm piece fresh
  ginger, julienned
1 long green chilli,
  seeded and julienned
2 spring onions, thinly
  sliced on the diagonal
1/4 cup (7 g) fresh
  coriander leaves
1/4 cup (60 ml) peanut
  oil
lime wedges, to serve

1. Fill a wok one third
full of water. Make
3 diagonal cuts on each
side of the fish through
the thickest part of the
flesh and to the bone to
ensure even cooking.
Line a bamboo steamer
with baking paper, big
enough to fit the fish.
2. Open the cavity of
the fish and place half
the coriander sprigs on
the bottom, then top
with the lime slices and
the remaining coriander
sprigs. Place the fish on
the baking paper in the
bamboo steamer and
place over the wok.
Sprinkle the ginger
over the fish, then
cover and steam for
20–25 minutes, or
until the flesh flakes
with a fork.
3. Remove the fish
from the steamer and
place on an ovenproof
serving dish. Arrange
the chilli, spring onion
and coriander leaves
over the top. Heat the
oil in a clean, dry wok
until smoking, then
pour over the fish.
Serve immediately with
lime wedges.

NUTRITION PER SERVE
Protein 45 g; Fat 18 g;
Carbohydrate 0.5 g; Dietary
Fibre 0 g; Cholesterol
137 mg; 1452 kJ (347 cal)

Stir-fried chicken and lemon grass

Preparation time:
  15 minutes
Total cooking time:
  12 minutes
Serves 4

1 tablespoon fish sauce
3 teaspoons grated
  palm sugar
1 tablespoon peanut oil
2 teaspoons sesame oil
800 g chicken breast
  fillets, cut into strips
2 tablespoons finely
  chopped lemon grass,
  white part only
1 1/2 tablespoons
  julienned fresh ginger
2 cloves garlic, finely
  chopped
2 tablespoons fresh
  coriander leaves
2 limes, cut into wedges

1. Place the fish sauce
and palm sugar in a
small bowl and stir
until all the sugar has
dissolved.
2. Heat a large wok
until very hot, add half
the combined oils and
swirl to coat. Add half
the chicken and stir-fry
for 4 minutes, then
remove. Repeat with
the remaining oil and
chicken and remove.
Add the lemon grass,
ginger and garlic to the
wok, and stir-fry for
1–2 minutes, then
return all the chicken to
the wok and stir-fry for
2 minutes more.
3. Stir in the combined
fish sauce and palm
sugar. Scatter with the
coriander leaves and
serve immediately with
noodles or rice and the
lime wedges.

NUTRITION PER SERVE
Protein 45 g; Fat 15 g;
Carbohydrate 2 g; Dietary
Fibre 0 g; Cholesterol
100 mg; 1330 kJ (318 cal)

Whole steamed fish (top)
and Stir-fried chicken and lemon grass

Honey sesame prawns

Preparation time:
25 minutes
Total cooking time:
10 minutes
Serves 4–6

oil, for deep-frying
3 egg whites, beaten
  to form soft peaks
2 tablespoons cornflour
1 kg raw prawns, peeled,
  deveined, tails intact
3/4 cup (260 g) honey
1 teaspoon sweet chilli
  sauce
2 teaspoons lemon juice
2 tablespoons sesame
  seeds, toasted
2 spring onions, thinly
  sliced on the diagonal

1. Fill a wok one third
full of oil and heat until
a cube of bread browns
in 15 seconds. Place
the egg, cornflour and
1/4 teaspoon salt in
a bowl and whisk
until smooth. Dip the
prawns into the batter
up to the tail and
carefully lower into the
wok. Cook in batches
for 3–4 minutes, or
until golden brown.
Drain and keep warm.
2. Put the honey, sweet
chilli sauce, lemon juice
and 1 tablespoon water

in a saucepan and mix
well. Stir over medium
heat until the mixture
thickens slightly.
3. Place the prawns on
a serving dish and pour
on the honey sauce.
Sprinkle with the sesame
seeds and top with the
spring onion.

NUTRITION PER SERVE (6)
*Protein 37 g; Fat 10 g;
Carbohydrate 40 g; Dietary
Fibre 0.5 g; Cholesterol
250 mg; 1640 kJ (390 cal)*

Mie Goreng

Preparation time:
  20 minutes +
  10 minutes standing
Total cooking time:
  10 minutes
Serves 4

1/4 cup (60 ml) lime juice
11/2 tablespoons fish
  sauce
2 tablespoons palm
  sugar
1/4 cup (60 ml) kecap
  manis
300 g dried rice noodles
1 tablespoon peanut oil
1 tablespoon sesame oil
600 g chicken breast
  fillets, cut into bite-
  size strips
4 spring onions, chopped
4 cloves garlic, crushed
2 teaspoons finely
  chopped red chilli

11/2 cups (115 g)
  shredded white
  cabbage
2 tablespoons fried
  shallots (see Note)
3 tablespoons fresh
  coriander leaves
2 green chillies, thinly
  sliced

1. Mix together the
lime juice, fish sauce,
palm sugar and kecap
manis, stirring until all
the sugar has dissolved.
Cover the noodles with
warm water and leave
for 10 minutes, or until
soft. Drain.
2. Heat a wok until very
hot, add the combined
oils and swirl to coat.
Add the chicken in
2 batches and stir-fry
for 3 minutes, or until
almost cooked through.
Add the spring onion,
garlic and chilli, and
cook for 1 minute.
3. Add the cabbage and
stir-fry for 2 minutes,
or until tender. Stir in
the noodles and lime
juice mixture. Top
with the fried shallots
and coriander leaves
and serve with a small
bowl of sliced chilli.

NUTRITION PER SERVE
*Protein 37 g; Fat 13 g;
Carbohydrate 30 g; Dietary
Fibre 2.5 g; Cholesterol
75 mg; 1608 kJ (385 cal)*

Note: Fried shallots are
available at Asian
grocery stores.

*Honey sesame prawns (top)
and Mie Goreng*

Butter chicken

Preparation time:
10 minutes
Total cooking time:
35 minutes
Serves 4–6

2 tablespoons peanut oil
1 kg chicken thigh
  fillets, quartered
60 g butter
2 teaspoons garam
  masala
2 teaspoons sweet
  paprika
2 teaspoons ground
  coriander
1 tablespoon finely
  chopped fresh ginger
1/4 teaspoon chilli
  powder
1 cinnamon stick
6 cardamom pods,
  bruised
350 g puréed tomatoes
1 tablespoon sugar
1/4 cup (60 g) plain
  yoghurt
1/2 cup (125 ml) cream
1 tablespoon lemon juice

1. Heat a wok until very
hot, add 1 tablespoon
oil and swirl to coat.
Add half the chicken and
stir-fry for 4 minutes,
or until browned.
Remove. Add extra oil,
as needed, and stir-fry
the remaining chicken.
Remove.
2. Reduce the heat, add
the butter and melt. Add
the spices and stir-fry
for 1 minute, or until
fragrant. Return the
chicken to the wok and
coat in the spices.
3. Add the tomato and
sugar, and simmer,
stirring, for 15 minutes,
or until the chicken is
tender and the sauce is
thick. Add the yoghurt,
cream and juice, and
stir-fry for 5 minutes,
or until the sauce has
thickened slightly.
Remove the cinnamon
and cardamom pods,
and serve with rice.

NUTRITION PER SERVE (6)
Protein 32 g; Fat 27 g;
Carbohydrate 7.5 g; Dietary
Fibre 1 g; Cholesterol
122 mg; 1669 kJ (397 cal)

Sichuan prawn stir-fry

Preparation time:
20 minutes
Total cooking time:
15 minutes
Serves 4

500 g Hokkien noodles
2 tablespoons oil
2 cloves garlic, sliced
1 onion, cut into thin
  wedges
1 tablespoon Sichuan
  peppercorns, crushed
1 stem lemon grass,
  white part only,
  finely chopped
300 g green beans, cut
  into 3 cm lengths
750 g raw large prawns,
  peeled, deveined,
  halved lengthways
2 tablespoons fish
  sauce
1/3 cup (80 ml) oyster
  sauce
1/2 cup (125 ml)
  chicken stock

1. Cover the noodles
with boiling water, stir
to separate, then drain.
2. Heat a wok until very
hot, add 1 tablespoon
oil and swirl to coat.
Add the garlic, onion,
peppercorns and lemon
grass, and stir-fry for
2 minutes, then add the
beans and stir-fry for
2–3 minutes, or until
tender. Remove.
3. Reheat the wok, add
the remaining oil and
swirl to coat. Add the
prawns and stir-fry for
3–4 minutes, or until
just cooked through.
Add the bean mixture
and noodles, and stir-fry
for 3 minutes, or until
the noodles are heated
through. Add the
sauces and stock, and
bring to the boil. Toss
well and serve.

NUTRITION PER SERVE
Protein 57 g; Fat 13 g;
Carbohydrate 92 g; Dietary
Fibre 6 g; Cholesterol
300 mg; 3013 kJ (720 cal)

Butter chicken (top)
and Sichuan prawn stir-fry

Fried rice

Preparation time:
10 minutes
Total cooking time:
5 minutes
Serves 4–6

1/4 cup (60 ml) peanut
  oil
2 eggs, beaten
1 1/2 cups (220 g) finely
  diced ham
100 g cooked prawns,
  finely chopped
4 cups (740 g) cold
  cooked rice
1/4 cup (40 g) frozen
  peas
1/4 cup (60 ml) light
  soy sauce
6 spring onions, thinly
  sliced on the diagonal

1. Heat a wok until very
hot, add 1 tablespoon
oil and swirl to coat.
Add the egg and start
to scramble. When
almost cooked, remove
from the wok and set
aside. Heat the
remaining oil in the
wok, then add the ham
and prawns, tossing to
heat through evenly.
2. Add the rice and
peas, toss and stir-fry
for 3 minutes, or until
the rice grains separate.
Add the scrambled egg,
sprinkle with the soy

sauce and toss to coat
the rice. Add the spring
onion, stir-fry for
2 minutes and serve.

NUTRITION PER SERVE (6)
*Protein 30 g; Fat 20 g;
Carbohydrate 148 g; Dietary
Fibre 5 g; Cholesterol
110 mg; 3728 kJ (890 cal)*

Beef with black
bean sauce

Preparation time:
15 minutes
Total cooking time:
20 minutes
Serves 4–6

2 tablespoons canned
  salted black beans
1 tablespoon dark soy
  sauce
1 tablespoon Chinese
  rice wine
1 clove garlic, finely
  chopped
1 teaspoon sugar
1/4 cup (60 ml) peanut
  oil
1 onion, cut into
  wedges
500 g lean rump or
  fillet steak, thinly
  sliced
1/2 teaspoon finely
  chopped fresh ginger
1 teaspoon cornflour,
  combined with
  1 tablespoon water
1 teaspoon sesame
  oil

1. Rinse the black
beans, drain and chop.
Place the soy sauce,
rice wine and 1/4 cup
(60 ml) water in a small
bowl, mix well and add
the beans. In a separate
bowl, crush the garlic
and sugar with a fork
to a smooth paste.
2. Heat a wok until very
hot, add 1 teaspoon
peanut oil and swirl
to coat. Add the
onion and stir-fry for
1–2 minutes. Remove.
Add 1 tablespoon
peanut oil and swirl
to coat. Add half
the beef and stir-fry
for 5–6 minutes, or
until browned.
Remove. Repeat with
the remaining beef.
Remove.
3. Add the remaining
peanut oil to the wok
with the garlic paste
and ginger, and stir-fry
for 30 seconds, or
until fragrant. Add the
bean mixture, onion
and beef. Bring to the
boil, then reduce the
heat and simmer,
covered, for 2 minutes.
Stir in the cornflour
mixture and stir until
the sauce boils and
thickens. Stir in the
sesame oil. Serve
with steamed rice.

NUTRITION PER SERVE (6)
*Protein 20 g; Fat 12 g;
Carbohydrate 4.5 g; Dietary
Fibre 1.5 g; Cholesterol
55 mg; 848 kJ (202 cal)*

*Fried rice (top)
and Beef with black bean sauce*

Spiced cauliflower and peas

Preparation time:
15 minutes
Total cooking time:
10 minutes
Serves 4–6

2 tablespoons oil
1 small onion, finely
   chopped
2 teaspoons yellow
   mustard seeds
3 cloves garlic, crushed
1 tablespoon finely
   chopped fresh ginger
1 tablespoon ground
   cumin
2 teaspoons ground
   coriander
2 teaspoons ground
   turmeric
1 small head (800 g)
   cauliflower, cut
   into florets
1 cup (155 g) frozen
   peas
*1/4 cup (15 g) chopped
   fresh coriander leaves*

1. Heat a wok until
very hot, add the oil
and swirl to coat. Add
the onion and mustard
seeds, and stir-fry for
2 minutes, or until the
mustard seeds pop.
2. Add the garlic,
ginger, cumin,
coriander, turmeric and
1 teaspoon salt, and
stir-fry for 1 minute, or
until fragrant. Add the
cauliflower and stir-fry

to coat with the spices.
3. Stir in 1 cup (250 ml)
water, cover and cook
for 4 minutes. Add
the peas and stir-fry
for 2–3 minutes, or
until the peas are
cooked and the
cauliflower is tender
but still crisp. Remove
from the heat and stir
in the coriander.

NUTRITION PER SERVE (6)
*Protein 5 g; Fat 7 g;
Carbohydrate 5 g; Dietary
Fibre 4.5 g; Cholesterol
0 mg; 418 kJ (100 cal)*

Warm curried chicken salad

Preparation time:
15 minutes +
   overnight marinating
Total cooking time:
10 minutes
Serves 4–6

3 tablespoons mild
   Indian curry paste
*1/4 cup (60 ml) coconut
   milk*
750 g chicken breast
   fillets, sliced
150 g green beans,
   halved
2 tablespoons peanut oil
*1/3 cup (25 g) flaked
   almonds, toasted*
1 red capsicum, sliced
240 g fresh rocket
100 g fried egg noodles

Lemon dressing
1/3 cup (80 ml) olive oil
2 tablespoons lemon
   juice
2 cloves garlic, crushed
1 teaspoon soft brown
   sugar

1. Place the curry paste
and coconut milk in a
bowl and mix together
well. Add the chicken,
toss to coat, cover and
refrigerate overnight.
2. Cook the beans
in boiling water for
30 seconds, or until
just tender. Refresh
under cold running
water. Drain.
3. Heat a wok until very
hot, add half the oil
and swirl to coat. Add
half the chicken and
stir-fry for 5 minutes,
or until cooked through.
Remove. Repeat with
the remaining chicken
and oil. Remove.
4. To make the dressing,
place the ingredients
in a jar and shake
to combine.
5. Place the chicken,
beans, almonds,
capsicum, rocket and
dressing in a large bowl,
and mix well. Stir in
the noodles and serve.

NUTRITION PER SERVE (6)
*Protein 32 g; Fat 29 g;
Carbohydrate 6.5 g; Dietary
Fibre 2.5 g; Cholesterol
72 mg; 1730 kJ (412 cal)*

*Spiced cauliflower and peas (top)
and Warm curried chicken salad*

Pull back the apron and remove the top shell from the crab.

Remove the intestines and grey feathery gills and segment into 4 pieces.

Chilli crab

Preparation time:
  20 minutes
Total cooking time:
  15 minutes
Serves 4

1 kg raw blue swimmer
  crabs
2 tablespoons peanut oil
2 cloves garlic, finely
  chopped
2 teaspoons finely
  chopped fresh ginger
2 red chillies, seeded
  and sliced
2 tablespoons hoisin
  sauce
1/2 cup (125 ml)
  tomato sauce
1/4 cup (60 ml) sweet
  chilli sauce
1 tablespoon fish sauce
1/2 teaspoon sesame oil
4 spring onions, sliced
fresh coriander sprigs,
  to garnish

1. Pull back the apron and remove the top shell from the crabs. Remove the intestines and grey feathery gills. Segment each crab into 4 pieces. Use a cracker to crack the claws open; this will make it easier to eat later and will also allow the flavours to get into the crab meat.
2. Heat a wok until very hot, add the oil and swirl to coat. Add the garlic, ginger and chilli, and stir-fry for 1–2 minutes.
3. Add the crab pieces and stir-fry for 5–7 minutes, or until they turn orange. Stir in the hoisin, tomato, sweet chilli and fish sauces, the sesame oil and 1/4 cup (60 ml) water. Bring to the boil, then reduce the heat and simmer,

covered, for 6 minutes, or until the crab shell turns bright orange and the flesh turns white and flakes easily.
4. Sprinkle with the spring onion and serve on a platter, garnished with the coriander sprigs. Serve with boiled rice.

NUTRITION PER SERVE
Protein 33 g; Fat 12 g; Carbohydrate 20 g; Dietary Fibre 3 g; Cholesterol 210 mg; 1310 kJ (313 cal)

Variation: You can use any variety of raw crab for this recipe, or substitute the crabs for raw prawns or Balmain bugs.
Note: The seeds and membrane contribute most of the hotness in chillies, so leave them in if you prefer a hotter sauce. Wear gloves to protect your hands from the heat of the chillies.

Chilli crab

Crack the claws open with a cracker to make the crab easier to eat.

Stir-fry the crab pieces until the shell turns orange.

Ma Por tofu

Preparation time:
  15 minutes +
  10 minutes marinating
Total cooking time:
  15 minutes
Serves 4

3 teaspoons cornflour
2 teaspoons soy sauce
1 teaspoon oyster sauce
1 clove garlic, finely
  chopped
250 g pork mince
1 tablespoon oil
3 teaspoons red bean
  chilli paste
3 teaspoons preserved
  bean curd
750 g firm tofu,
  drained, cubed
2 spring onions, sliced
3 teaspoons oyster
  sauce, extra
2 teaspoons soy sauce,
  extra
1¹/₂ teaspoons sugar

1. Put the cornflour,
soy and oyster sauces
and the garlic in a bowl,
and mix well. Add the
mince, toss to coat and
leave for 10 minutes.
2. Heat a wok until
very hot, add the oil
and swirl to coat. Add
the mince and stir-fry
for 5 minutes, or until
browned. Add the chilli
paste and bean curd,
and cook for 2 minutes,
or until fragrant.
3. Add the remaining

ingredients and stir
for 3–5 minutes, or
until the tofu is heated
through. Serve with rice.

NUTRITION PER SERVE
*Protein 26 g; Fat 12 g;
Carbohydrate 5 g; Dietary
Fibre 0 g; Cholesterol
30 mg; 1092 kJ (260 cal)*

Sesame pork

Preparation time:
  10 minutes
Total cooking time:
  20 minutes
Serves 4

2 tablespoons sesame
  seeds
3 tablespoons peanut oil
600 g pork fillets,
  thinly sliced
2 tablespoons hoisin
  sauce
2 tablespoons teriyaki
  sauce
2 teaspoons cornflour
2 teaspoons sesame oil
8 spring onions, sliced
  on the diagonal
2 cloves garlic, crushed
2 teaspoons finely
  grated fresh ginger
2 carrots, julienned
200 g snake beans, cut
  into 6 cm lengths

1. Preheat the oven to
moderate 180°C (350°F/
Gas 4). Place the sesame
seeds on an oven tray

and bake for 5 minutes,
or until browned.
2. Heat a wok until very
hot, add 1 tablespoon
oil and swirl to coat.
Add half the pork and
stir-fry for 3 minutes,
or until browned.
Remove. Repeat with
the remaining pork.
Remove.
3. Combine the hoisin
and teriyaki sauces,
cornflour and
1 tablespoon water.
4. Reheat the wok until
very hot, add the
remaining peanut oil
and the sesame oil and
swirl to coat. Add the
spring onion, garlic and
ginger, and stir-fry for
1 minute, or until
fragrant.
5. Add the carrot and
beans, and stir-fry for
3 minutes, or until
almost cooked but
still crunchy. Return
the pork to the wok,
add the cornflour
mixture and stir until
the sauce boils and
thickens. Simmer until
the meat is tender and
the vegetables are just
cooked. Toss through
the sesame seeds. Serve
with boiled rice.

NUTRITION PER SERVE
*Protein 38 g; Fat 27 g;
Carbohydrate 7.5 g; Dietary
Fibre 4.5 g; Cholesterol
75 mg; 1766 kJ (420 cal)*

*Ma Por tofu (top)
and Sesame pork*

Green fish curry

Preparation time:
15 minutes
Total cooking time:
15 minutes
Serves 4

1 tablespoon peanut oil
1 brown onion, chopped
1–1^1/$_2$ tablespoons
  green curry paste
1^1/$_2$ cups (375 ml)
  coconut milk
700 g firm white
  boneless fish fillets,
  cut into bite-size pieces
3 kaffir lime leaves
1 tablespoon fish sauce
2 teaspoons grated
  palm sugar
2 tablespoons lime juice
1 green chilli, finely
  sliced

1. Heat a wok until very
hot, add the peanut oil
and swirl to coat. Add
the onion and stir-fry
for 2 minutes, or until
soft. Add the curry
paste and stir-fry for
2 minutes, or until
fragrant. Stir in the
coconut milk and bring
to the boil.
2. Add the fish and
lime leaves, reduce the
heat and simmer,
stirring occasionally,
for 8–10 minutes, or
until the fish is cooked
through. Stir in the fish
sauce, palm sugar and
lime juice. Scatter with
the chilli and serve
with boiled rice.

NUTRITION PER SERVE
*Protein 40 g; Fat 30 g;
Carbohydrate 5.5 g; Dietary
Fibre 2 g; Cholesterol
125 mg; 1850 kJ (442 cal)*

Chicken and
eggplant red curry

Preparation time:
15 minutes + standing
Total cooking time:
35 minutes
Serves 4

500 g eggplant, cut into
  2 cm cubes
^{1}/$_4$ cup (60 ml) peanut
  oil
500 g chicken breast
  fillets, cut into
  2 cm cubes
4 spring onions, chopped
2^1/$_2$ tablespoons red
  curry paste
1 cup (250 ml) coconut
  cream
^{1}/$_2$ cup (125 ml)
  chicken stock
4 kaffir lime leaves,
  shredded
3 teaspoons grated
  palm sugar
2 tablespoons fish sauce
2 tablespoons fresh
  Vietnamese mint
  leaves

1. Place the eggplant in
a shallow bowl and
sprinkle with salt.
Leave for 30 minutes,
then rinse and drain
thoroughly.
2. Heat a wok until very
hot, add 1 tablespoon
peanut oil and swirl to
coat. Add half the
chicken and stir-fry for
4 minutes, or until
browned. Remove. Add
another tablespoon oil
and the rest of the
chicken, and stir-fry.
Remove. Heat the
remaining oil, add the
eggplant and spring
onion, and stir-fry for
3–4 minutes.
3. Return the chicken
to the wok and add the
curry paste. Cook,
stirring, over high heat
for 1 minute, or until
fragrant. Add the
coconut cream, stock,
lime leaves, palm
sugar and fish sauce,
and bring to the boil.
Reduce the heat
and simmer for
15–20 minutes, or
until the eggplant and
chicken are tender
and cooked through.
4. Season to taste with
salt and scatter the
Vietnamese mint leaves
over the top. Serve with
boiled rice.

NUTRITION PER SERVE
*Protein 32 g; Fat 30 g;
Carbohydrate 8.8 g; Dietary
Fibre 4.5 g; Cholesterol
63 mg; 1842 kJ (440 cal)*

*Green fish curry (top)
and Chicken and eggplant red curry*

Stir-fried tofu and bok choy

Preparation time:
  20 minutes +
  10 minutes marinating
Total cooking time:
  10 minutes
Serves 4

600 g firm tofu, cubed
1 tablespoon finely
  chopped fresh ginger
2 tablespoons soy sauce
2 tablespoons peanut oil
1 red onion, finely sliced
4 cloves garlic, crushed
500 g baby bok choy,
  sliced into strips
  lengthways
2 teaspoons sesame oil
2 tablespoons kecap
  manis
1/4 cup (60 ml) sweet
  chilli sauce
1 tablespoon toasted
  sesame seeds

1. Put the tofu in a bowl with the ginger. Pour in the soy sauce and leave for 10 minutes. Drain.
2. Heat a wok until very hot, add half the oil and swirl to coat. Add the onion and stir-fry for 3 minutes, or until soft. Add the tofu and garlic, and stir-fry for 3 minutes, or until golden. Remove and keep warm.
3. Reheat the wok until very hot, add the remaining oil and swirl to coat. Add the bok choy and stir-fry for 2 minutes, or until wilted. Return the tofu mixture to the wok.
4. Stir in the sesame oil, kecap manis and chilli sauce. Scatter with the sesame seeds and serve with rice noodles.

NUTRITION PER SERVE
Protein 18.5 g; Fat 20 g; Carbohydrate 7 g; Dietary Fibre 7 g; Cholesterol 0 mg; 1232 kJ (293 cal)

Satay lamb

Preparation time:
  10 minutes
Total cooking time:
  15 minutes
Serves 4

1/4 cup (60 ml) peanut oil
750 g lamb backstraps,
  thinly sliced
2 teaspoons ground
  cumin
1 teaspoon ground
  turmeric
1 red capsicum, sliced
1/4 cup (60 ml) sweet
  chilli sauce
1/4 cup (60 g) crunchy
  peanut butter
1 cup (250 ml) coconut
  milk
2 teaspoons soft brown
  sugar
1–2 tablespoons lemon
  juice, to taste
1/3 cup (10 g) chopped
  fresh coriander leaves
1/4 cup (40 g) unsalted
  peanuts, roasted,
  chopped, to serve

1. Heat a wok until very hot, add 1 tablespoon oil and swirl to coat. Add half the lamb and stir-fry for 3 minutes, or until browned. Remove. Repeat with another tablespoon oil and the remaining lamb.
2. Reheat the wok, add the remaining oil and swirl to coat. Add the cumin, turmeric and capsicum, and stir-fry for 2 minutes, or until the capsicum is tender.
3. Return the lamb to the wok. Stir in the chilli sauce, peanut butter, coconut milk and sugar. Bring to the boil, then reduce the heat and simmer for 5 minutes, or until the meat is tender and the sauce has thickened slightly. Remove from the heat and add the lemon juice. Stir in the coriander and sprinkle with the peanuts. Serve with boiled rice.

NUTRITION PER SERVE
Protein 50 g; Fat 45 g; Carbohydrate 10 g; Dietary Fibre 4.5 g; Cholesterol 125 mg; 2710 kJ (645 cal)

Stir-fried tofu and bok choy (top) and Satay lamb

Laksa lemak

Preparation time:
1 hour +
20 minutes soaking
Total cooking time:
1 hour 20 minutes
Serves 4

4–5 large dried red
  chillies
500 g raw King prawns
1/3 cup (80 ml) oil
1 red onion, roughly
  chopped
5 cm piece galangal,
  peeled and roughly
  chopped
4 stems lemon grass,
  white part only, sliced
3 red chillies, seeded
  and roughly chopped
10 candlenuts (see Note)
2 teaspoons shrimp
  paste
2 teaspoons grated
  fresh turmeric
2 cups (500 ml)
  coconut milk
8 ready-made fried fish
  balls, sliced (see Note)
500 g fresh rice noodles
1–2 Lebanese
  cucumbers, julienned
100 g bean sprouts
2 tablespoons fresh
  Vietnamese mint
  leaves

1. Put the chillies in a
heatproof bowl, cover
with hot water and
soak for 20 minutes.

2. Set aside 4 prawns
and peel the remainder,
retaining all the heads
and shells. Heat a wok
until very hot, add
1 tablespoon oil and
swirl to coat. Add
the heads and shells,
and stir-fry for about
10 minutes, or until
aromatic and bright,
dark orange in colour.
Stir in 1 cup (250 ml)
water and, when it has
almost evaporated, add
another cup (250 ml)
water and bring to the
boil. Add 1 litre water
to the wok, bring to the
boil again, then reduce
the heat and simmer for
30 minutes.
3. Drain the chillies
and place in a food
processor with the
onion, galangal, lemon
grass, fresh chilli,
candlenuts, shrimp
paste, turmeric and
2 tablespoons oil.
Process until finely
chopped.
4. Add the 4 reserved
whole prawns to the
wok and cook for
10 minutes, or until
they turn pink. Remove
the prawns and strain
the stock, discarding
the shells. There should
be about 2–3 cups
(500–750 ml) stock.
5. Heat a clean wok
until very hot, add the
remaining tablespoon

oil and swirl to coat.
Add the spice paste,
reduce the heat to
low and cook, stirring,
for 8 minutes, or
until the mixture is
very aromatic. Stir in
the stock and coconut
milk. Bring to the
boil, then reduce the
heat and simmer for
5 minutes. Add the
prawn meat and fish
ball slices, and simmer
for 2–3 minutes, or
until the prawns
turn pink.
6. Bring a separate
saucepan of water to
the boil, add the
noodles and cook for
30 seconds, without
overcooking. Drain
and divide among
4 deep soup bowls.
7. Ladle the soup over
the noodles. Garnish
with cucumber, bean
sprouts and mint, and
top with a whole
prawn. Serve
immediately.

NUTRITION PER SERVE
*Protein 35 g; Fat 50 g;
Carbohydrate 35 g; Dietary
Fibre 5 g; Cholesterol
200 mg; 3032 kJ (725 cal)*

Note: Ready-made fish
balls and candlenuts
are available from
Asian grocery stores.
Candlenuts are thought
to be toxic if uncooked.
If you prefer, you can
use macadamia nuts
instead.

Laksa lemak

Barbecue pork with Asian greens

Preparation time:
10 minutes
Total cooking time:
10 minutes
Serves 4

1.6 kg Chinese broccoli,
  cut into 5 cm lengths
1 tablespoon peanut oil
2 cm piece fresh ginger,
  julienned
2 cloves garlic, crushed
500 g Chinese barbecue
  pork, thinly sliced
1/4 cup (60 ml) chicken
  or vegetable stock
1/4 cup (60 ml) oyster
  sauce
1 tablespoon kecap
  manis

1. Place the broccoli
in a steamer over a
saucepan or wok of
simmering water and
cook for 5 minutes, or
until just tender but
still crisp.
2. Heat a wok until very
hot, add the oil and
swirl to coat. Add the
ginger and garlic, and
stir-fry for 30 seconds,
or until fragrant. Add
the broccoli and pork,
and toss to coat.
3. Pour in the combined
stock, oyster sauce
and kecap manis, and
stir-fry until heated
through. Serve with
rice or noodles.

NUTRITION PER SERVE
*Protein 30 g; Fat 7 g;
Carbohydrate 4.5 g; Dietary
Fibre 2 g; Cholesterol
60 mg; 886 kJ (212 cal)*

Caramel coriander chicken

Preparation time:
20 minutes +
  overnight refrigeration
Total cooking time:
20 minutes
Serves 4–6

2 teaspoons ground
  turmeric
6 cloves garlic, crushed
2 tablespoons finely
  minced fresh ginger
2 tablespoons soy sauce
1/4 cup (60 ml) Chinese
  rice wine or sherry
2 egg yolks, beaten
1 kg chicken thigh fillets,
  cut into 2 cm cubes
1/2 cup (60 g) plain
  flour
1/2 cup (125 ml) oil
1/2 cup (95 g) soft
  brown sugar
1/3 cup (20 g) chopped
  fresh coriander
1/4 cup (60 ml) rice
  vinegar

1. Place the turmeric,
two crushed garlic
cloves, the ginger, soy,
rice wine, egg yolks,
1 teaspoon salt and
1 teaspoon white
pepper in a large bowl,
and mix together well.
Add the chicken and
toss to coat. Cover with
plastic wrap and
refrigerate overnight.
2. Remove any excess
liquid from the chicken,
add the flour and toss
to mix well.
3. Heat a wok until very
hot, add 1 tablespoon
oil and swirl to coat.
Add a third of the
chicken and stir-fry for
4 minutes, or until
golden brown. Remove
from the wok. Repeat
this step twice with the
remaining chicken.
Remove and keep warm.
4. Reduce the heat to
medium, add the
remaining oil, brown
sugar and remaining
garlic. Mix together
and then leave for
1–2 minutes, or until
the sugar caramelises
and liquefies.
5. Return the chicken
to the wok, and add
the coriander and
vinegar. Stir gently
for 4 minutes, or until
the chicken is cooked
through and well
coated with the sauce.
Serve with boiled rice.

NUTRITION PER SERVE (6)
*Protein 35 g; Fat 25 g;
Carbohydrate 30 g; Dietary
Fibre 2 g; Cholesterol
130 mg; 2070 kJ (495 cal)*

*Barbecue pork with Asian greens (top)
and Caramel coriander chicken*

Vietnamese chicken salad

Preparation time:
25 minutes
Total cooking time:
10 minutes
Serves 6

1 small Chinese cabbage,
  finely shredded
2 tablespoons oil
2 onions, halved and
  sliced thinly
500 g chicken thigh
  fillets, trimmed and
  cut into strips
1/4 cup (60 g) sugar
1/4 cup (60 ml) fish sauce
1/3 cup (80 ml) lime juice
1 tablespoon white
  vinegar
2/3 cup (30 g) chopped
  fresh Vietnamese mint
  or mint
2/3 cup (30 g) chopped
  fresh coriander
fresh Vietnamese
  mint leaves, extra,
  to garnish

1. Place the cabbage in
a large bowl, cover with
plastic wrap and chill.
2. Heat a wok until very
hot, add 1 tablespoon
oil and swirl to coat.
Add half the onion and
half the chicken, and
stir-fry for 4–5 minutes,
or until the chicken is
cooked through.

Remove and repeat with
the remaining oil, onion
and chicken. Cool.
3. To make the
dressing, put the sugar,
fish sauce, lime juice,
vinegar and 1/2 teaspoon
salt in a small jug, and
mix well. To serve, toss
together the cabbage,
chicken and onion,
dressing, mint and
coriander and garnish
with the mint leaves.

NUTRITION PER SERVE
*Protein 17 g; Fat 8 g;
Carbohydrate 13 g; Dietary
Fibre 1.5 g; Cholesterol
35 mg; 805 kJ (190 cal)*

Thai beef salad

Preparation time:
20 minutes + cooling
Total cooking time:
5 minutes
Serves 6

2 tablespoons peanut oil
500 g beef fillet or lean
  rump, thinly sliced
2 cloves garlic, crushed
1/4 cup (15 g) finely
  chopped fresh
  coriander roots
  and stems
1 tablespoon grated
  palm sugar
1/3 cup (80 ml) lime juice
2 tablespoons fish sauce
2 small red chillies,
  seeded, finely sliced

2 red Asian shallots,
  finely sliced
2 telegraph cucumbers,
  sliced into thin ribbons
1 cup (20 g) fresh mint
  leaves
1 cup (90 g) bean sprouts
1/4 cup (40 g) chopped
  roasted peanuts

1. Heat a wok until very
hot, add half the oil
and swirl to coat. Add
half the beef and cook
for 1–2 minutes, or until
medium rare. Remove.
Repeat with the
remaining oil and beef.
2. Place the garlic,
coriander, palm sugar,
lime juice, fish sauce,
1/4 teaspoon ground
white pepper and
1/4 teaspoon salt in a
bowl, and stir until all
the sugar has dissolved.
Add the chilli and
shallots, and mix well.
3. Pour the sauce over
the beef while still hot,
mix well, then cool to
room temperature.
4. In a separate bowl,
toss together the
cucumber and mint
leaves, and refrigerate
until required.
5. Place the cucumber
and mint on a serving
platter, and top with
the beef, bean sprouts
and peanuts.

NUTRITION PER SERVE
*Protein 22 g; Fat 13 g;
Carbohydrate 7.5 g; Dietary
Fibre 2 g; Cholesterol
50 mg; 1041 kJ (248 cal)*

*Vietnamese chicken salad (top)
and Thai beef salad*

Duck and pineapple curry

Preparation time:
10 minutes
Total cooking time:
15 minutes
Serves 4–6

1 tablespoon peanut oil
8 spring onions, sliced
  into 3 cm lengths
2 cloves garlic, crushed
1 tablespoon red curry
  paste, or to taste
750 g Chinese barbecue
  duck, chopped
400 ml coconut milk
450 g can pineapple
  pieces in syrup, drained
3 kaffir lime leaves
1/4 cup (15 g) chopped
  fresh coriander
2 tablespoons chopped
  fresh mint

1. Heat a wok until
very hot, add the oil
and swirl to coat. Add
the spring onion, garlic
and curry paste, and
stir-fry for 1 minute, or
until fragrant.
2. Add the remaining
ingredients. Bring to
the boil, then reduce
the heat and simmer for
10 minutes, or until the
duck is heated through.
Serve with jasmine rice.

NUTRITION PER SERVE (6)
*Protein 4 g; Fat 32 g;
Carbohydrate 25 g; Dietary
Fibre 4.5 g; Cholesterol
10 mg; 1705 kJ (405 cal)*

Scallops with black bean sauce

Preparation time:
15 minutes
Total cooking time:
10 minutes
Serves 4–6

600 g large fresh
  scallops, without roe
2 tablespoons cornflour
1/3 cup (80 ml) peanut
  oil, plus 1 teaspoon,
  extra
3 spring onions, cut
  into 3 cm lengths
1 teaspoon finely
  chopped fresh ginger
2 cloves garlic,
  crushed
1/4 cup (55 g) dried
  black beans, lightly
  rinsed, roughly
  chopped
2 tablespoons Chinese
  rice wine
1 tablespoon rice wine
  vinegar
1 tablespoon soy
  sauce
1 teaspoon soft brown
  sugar
1/2 teaspoon sesame
  oil

1. Remove and discard
any veins, membrane
or hard white muscle
from the scallops. Toss
the scallops in the
cornflour to coat and
shake off any excess.
2. Heat a wok until very
hot, add 1 teaspoon
peanut oil and swirl to
coat. Add the spring
onion and stir-fry for
30 seconds, then
remove from the wok.
3. Add 1 tablespoon
peanut oil to the hot
wok and swirl to coat.
Add one third of the
scallops and stir-fry for
1–2 minutes, or until
golden and well sealed
—no liquid should be
released. Remove and
set aside. Repeat twice
more to seal the rest of
the scallops.
4. Add the remaining
tablespoon peanut oil
to the hot wok and
swirl to coat. Add the
ginger, garlic, black
beans, rice wine, rice
vinegar, soy sauce and
brown sugar, and stir-
fry for 1 minute, or
until the sauce boils
and thickens slightly.
5. Return the scallops
to the wok and stir-fry
for 1 minute, or until
heated through and
the sauce has thickened
again. Stir in the spring
onion and sesame oil.
Serve with boiled rice.

NUTRITION PER SERVE (6)
*Protein 15 g; Fat 15 g;
Carbohydrate 7 g; Dietary
Fibre 2 g; Cholesterol
33 mg; 917 kJ (220 cal)*

*Duck and pineapple curry (top)
and Scallops with black bean sauce*

Using a sharp knife, thinly slice the spring onions on the diagonal.

Cook the prawn heads and shells until deep red and aromatic.

Tom Yum Goong

Preparation time:
 35 minutes
Total cooking time:
 40 minutes
Serves 4–6

1 kg raw prawns
1/4 cup (60 ml) oil
2 stems lemon grass,
 white part only,
 bruised and sliced
 diagonally
1 litre fish stock
5 cm piece fresh ginger,
 thinly sliced
4 kaffir lime leaves
4–6 small red chillies,
 bruised
1 small onion, finely
 chopped
1 tablespoon sambal
 oelek
2 tablespoons tamarind
 concentrate
200 g button
 mushrooms

1 tomato, cut into
 8 wedges
2 spring onions,
 thinly sliced on
 the diagonal
1/3 cup (80 ml) lime
 juice
1–2 tablespoons fish
 sauce
1/2 cup (15 g) fresh
 coriander leaves

1. Peel and devein the
prawns, leaving the
tails intact. Retain the
heads and shells to
make the soup base.
2. Heat a wok until
very hot, add the oil
and swirl to coat. Add
the prawn heads and
shells, and cook for
8–10 minutes, or until
deep red and aromatic.
3. Add the lemon grass,
fish stock and 2 cups
(500 ml) water, and
simmer for 20 minutes.
Strain into a bowl,
reserving half the

lemon grass pieces but
discarding all of the
prawn heads and shells.
4. Return the liquid to
the wok and add the
lemon grass pieces,
ginger, lime leaves,
chillies and onion.
Bring to the boil, then
reduce the heat and
simmer for 2 minutes.
Add the sambal oelek,
tamarind concentrate
and mushrooms, and
simmer for 2 minutes.
5. Add the tomato,
spring onion and
prawns, and cook for
3–5 minutes, or until
the prawns are cooked
and tender.
6. Remove the wok
from the heat and stir
in the lime juice and
fish sauce to taste. Stir
in the coriander leaves
and serve immediately.

NUTRITION PER SERVE (6)
*Protein 36 g; Fat 11 g;
Carbohydrate 2 g; Dietary
Fibre 1.5 g; Cholesterol
248 mg; 1055 kJ (252 cal)*

Tom Yum Goong

*Add the lemon grass, ginger, lime leaves,
chillies and onion to the wok.*

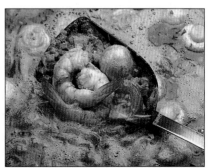

*Cook for 3–5 minutes more, or until the
prawns are cooked and tender.*

43

Chinese omelette

Preparation time:
  5 minutes
Total cooking time:
  5 minutes
Serves 4

*250 g cooked prawns
6 eggs
6 spring onions, finely
  sliced
2 tablespoons peanut oil
1 tablespoon light soy
  sauce
1 tablespoon oyster
  sauce
2 tablespoons dry sherry
1 tablespoon rice vinegar
1 teaspoon sugar
2 teaspoons finely
  shredded fresh ginger
1 tablespoon cornflour
2 teaspoons chopped
  fresh coriander leaves*

1. Shell, devein and
finely chop the prawns.
2. Whisk the eggs with
$1/2$ teaspoon salt and
$1/4$ teaspoon white
pepper. Add the prawns
and spring onion.
3. Heat a wok until hot,
add the oil and swirl to
coat. Pour in the egg
mixture and cook for
2 minutes, or until
puffed up and brown
underneath. Divide
into four and turn over
to cook the other side.
Remove and keep warm.
4. Add the soy and
oyster sauces, sherry,

rice vinegar, sugar,
ginger and $3/4$ cup
(185 ml) water to the
clean wok. Stir over
medium heat until the
sugar has dissolved,
then boil for 1 minute.
5. Blend the cornflour
and 2 tablespoons
water and stir into the
sauce until it boils and
thickens. Pour over the
omelette and sprinkle
with the coriander.

NUTRITION PER SERVE
*Protein 23 g; Fat 17 g;
Carbohydrate 6 g; Dietary
Fibre 0.5 g; Cholesterol
365 mg; 1175 kJ (280 cal)*

Lemon chicken

Preparation time:
  15 minutes
Total cooking time:
  20 minutes
Serves 4

*800 g chicken breast or
  thigh fillets, trimmed
1 egg, lightly beaten
cornflour, to coat
oil, for deep-frying
$1/2$ cup (125 ml) lemon
  juice
1 tablespoon white
  vinegar
$1/4$ cup (60 g) sugar
$1 1/2$ tablespoons
  cornflour
2 spring onions, sliced
lemon, to garnish*

1. Season the chicken
with salt and freshly
ground black pepper.
Coat with the egg, then
the cornflour, shaking
off any excess.
2. Fill a wok one third
full of oil and heat until
a cube of bread dropped
into the oil browns in
15 seconds. Add the
chicken in batches and
cook for 6 minutes, or
until golden brown
and cooked through.
Drain on crumpled
paper towels.
3. Combine the lemon
juice, vinegar, sugar
and $1/4$ cup (60 ml)
water in a small
saucepan, and stir over
low heat until the sugar
dissolves. Bring to the
boil, then reduce the
heat and simmer for
1–2 minutes. Combine
the cornflour with
$1/4$ cup (60 ml) water,
add to the pan and
mix well. Cook for
1 minute, or until
the sauce boils
and thickens.
4. To serve, slice the
chicken, spoon on the
sauce and garnish with
the spring onion and
lemon. Serve with rice.

NUTRITION PER SERVE
*Protein 47 g; Fat 15 g;
Carbohydrate 20 g; Dietary
Fibre 0 g; Cholesterol
145 mg; 1740 kJ (416 cal)*

*Chinese omelette (top)
and Lemon chicken*

Lemon grass prawns

Preparation time:
30 minutes
Total cooking time:
10 minutes
Serves 4

1 tablespoon peanut oil
2 cloves garlic, crushed
1 tablespoon finely
  grated fresh ginger
2 tablespoons finely
  chopped lemon grass,
  white part only
8 spring onions, cut
  into 4 cm pieces
1 kg raw prawns, peeled,
  deveined, tails intact
2 tablespoons lime juice
1 tablespoon soft
  brown sugar
2 teaspoons fish sauce
1/4 cup (60 ml) chicken
  stock
1 teaspoon cornflour
500 g baby bok choy,
  cut in half lengthways
1/4 cup (15 g) chopped
  fresh mint

1. Heat a wok until very
hot, add the oil and
swirl to coat. Add the
garlic, ginger, lemon
grass and spring onion,
and stir-fry for 1 minute,
or until fragrant. Add
the prawns and stir-fry
for 2 minutes.
2. Place the lime juice,

sugar, fish sauce,
chicken stock and
cornflour in a small
bowl. Mix well, then
add to the wok and
stir until the sauce boils
and thickens. Cook for
a further 1–2 minutes,
or until the prawns are
pink and just tender.
3. Add the bok choy
and stir-fry for 1 minute,
or until wilted. Stir in
the mint and serve.

NUTRITION PER SERVE
*Protein 60 g; Fat 8.5 g;
Carbohydrate 8 g; Dietary
Fibre 1.6 g; Cholesterol
373 mg; 1433 kJ (342 cal)*

Thai Musaman beef curry

Preparation time:
20 minutes
Total cooking time:
1 hour 45 minutes
Serves 6–8

1 kg blade steak, cut
  into 5 cm cubes
4 cardamom pods,
  bruised
2 stems lemon grass,
  white part only,
  chopped
2 cups (500 ml)
  coconut milk
3 tablespoons Thai
  Musaman curry paste
2 large potatoes, cut
  into 3 cm cubes

10 small pickling onions
2 tablespoons fish sauce
1/4 cup (60 ml) lime
  juice
2 tablespoons palm sugar
2 tablespoons tamarind
  concentrate
10 fresh Thai basil
  leaves, shredded
1/2 cup (80 g) whole
  roasted peanuts

1. Place the beef in a
saucepan with the
cardamom pods,
lemon grass, 1 1/2 cups
(375 ml) coconut milk,
1 cup (250 ml) water
and 1 teaspoon salt.
Bring to the boil, then
reduce the heat and
simmer, covered, for
1 hour, or until the
meat is tender.
2. Place the remaining
coconut milk in a wok
and stir over medium
heat until thick and oily.
Add the curry paste
and cook for 3 minutes,
or until fragrant.
3. Add the meat, and its
cooking liquid, potato,
onions, fish sauce, lime
juice, palm sugar and
tamarind. Simmer for
30–40 minutes, or until
the potato is tender.
4. Stir in the basil and
peanuts, and simmer
for 2 minutes. Serve
with boiled rice.

NUTRITION PER SERVE (8)
*Protein 40 g; Fat 30 g;
Carbohydrate 17 g; Dietary
Fibre 3 g; Cholesterol
85 mg; 2070 kJ (495 cal)*

*Lemon grass prawns (top)
and Thai Musaman beef curry*

Sweet chilli squid

Preparation time:
 20 minutes
Total cooking time:
 10 minutes
Serves 4

750 g squid hoods
1 tablespoon peanut oil
1 tablespoon finely
 grated fresh ginger
2 cloves garlic, crushed
8 spring onions, chopped
2 tablespoons sweet
 chilli sauce
2 tablespoons Chinese
 barbecue sauce
1 tablespoon soy sauce
550 g bok choy, cut
 into 3 cm pieces
1 tablespoon chopped
 fresh coriander leaves

1. Cut the squid hoods open, score diagonal slashes across the inside surface and cut into 2 x 9 cm pieces.
2. Heat a wok until very hot, add the oil and swirl to coat. Add the ginger, garlic, spring onion and squid, and stir-fry for 3 minutes, or until browned.
3. Add the sauces and 2 tablespoons water to the wok, and stir-fry for 2 minutes, or until the squid is just tender. Add the bok choy and coriander, and stir-fry for 1 minute, or until the bok choy is tender.

NUTRITION PER SERVE
Protein 40 g; Fat 8 g; Carbohydrate 4 g; Dietary Fibre 7.5 g; Cholesterol 375 mg; 1030 kJ (245 cal)

Sichuan pork with capsicum

Preparation time:
 30 minutes
Total cooking time:
 10 minutes
Serves 4–6

1 1/2 tablespoons
 cornflour
1 tablespoon Sichuan
 peppercorns, ground
2 egg whites, beaten
500 g pork fillet, thinly
 sliced
2 tablespoons peanut
 oil, plus 1 teaspoon,
 extra
1 red capsicum, thinly
 sliced
2 spring onions, sliced
 into 3 cm lengths
2 teaspoons chilli oil
4 star anise
2 cloves garlic,
 crushed
2 teaspoons finely
 chopped fresh ginger
2 tablespoons oyster
 sauce
2 tablespoons Chinese
 rice wine
2 tablespoons soy sauce
1/2 teaspoon sesame
 oil
2 teaspoons sugar

1. Place the cornflour, peppercorns, egg whites and 1/2 teaspoon salt in a bowl. Mix well, then add the pork and toss to coat.
2. Heat a wok until very hot, add 1 teaspoon peanut oil and swirl to coat. Add the capsicum and spring onion, and stir-fry for 1 minute. Remove from the wok.
3. Add 1 tablespoon peanut oil to the wok and swirl to coat. Add half the pork and stir-fry for 2 minutes, or until sealed. Remove. Repeat with the remaining oil and pork.
4. Add the chilli oil to the wok and swirl to coat. Add the star anise and stir-fry for 30 seconds, then add the garlic and ginger, and stir-fry for another few seconds.
5. Combine the oyster sauce, rice wine, soy sauce, sesame oil and sugar, add to the wok and cook for 30 seconds. Return the pork to the wok and stir-fry for 1 minute, then stir in the vegetables and serve.

NUTRITION PER SERVE (6)
Protein 20 g; Fat 11 g; Carbohydrate 4 g; Dietary Fibre 0.5 g; Cholesterol 40 mg; 865 kJ (207 cal)

*Sweet chilli squid (top)
and Sichuan pork with capsicum*

Prawn salad with kaffir lime

Preparation time:
  20 minutes
Total cooking time:
  8 minutes
Serves 4

750 g raw large prawns
1 tablespoon oil
4 spring onions, cut
  into 3 cm lengths
1 small red chilli,
  seeded, finely chopped
2 cloves garlic, sliced
2 kaffir lime leaves,
  finely shredded
3 teaspoons grated
  fresh ginger
3 teaspoons soft brown
  sugar
2 teaspoons soy sauce
2 tablespoons mirin
2 tablespoons lime juice
2 cups (70 g) mixed
  lettuce leaves

1. Peel and devein the prawns, and cut in half lengthways. Heat a wok until very hot, add half the oil and swirl to coat. Add the prawns and stir-fry for 3 minutes, or until nearly cooked.
2. Add the spring onion, chilli, garlic, lime leaves and ginger. Stir-fry for 1–2 minutes, or until fragrant.

3. Combine the sugar, soy sauce, mirin and lime juice in a bowl, add to the wok and bring to the boil. Serve on the lettuce leaves.

NUTRITION PER SERVE
Protein 1 g; Fat 5 g; Carbohydrate 3.5 g; Dietary Fibre 1 g; Cholesterol 2 mg; 263 kJ (63 cal)

Nonya lime chicken

Preparation time:
  20 minutes
Total cooking time:
  25 minutes
Serves 4–6

2/3 cup (90 g) red Asian
  shallots
4 cloves garlic
2 stems lemon grass,
  white part only,
  chopped
2 teaspoons finely
  chopped fresh
  galangal
1 teaspoon ground
  turmeric
2 tablespoons sambal
  oelek
1 tablespoon shrimp
  paste
1/4 cup (60 ml) oil
1 kg chicken thigh
  fillets, cut into
  3 cm cubes
400 ml coconut
  milk

1 teaspoon finely
  grated lime rind
1/2 cup (125 ml) lime
  juice
6 kaffir lime leaves,
  finely shredded
2 tablespoons tamarind
  concentrate
lime wedges, to garnish
kaffir lime leaves,
  extra, to garnish

1. Place the shallots, garlic, lemon grass, galangal, turmeric, sambal oelek and shrimp paste in a blender and blend until smooth.
2. Heat a wok until very hot, add the oil and swirl to coat. Add the spice paste and stir-fry for 1–2 minutes, or until fragrant. Add the chicken and stir-fry for 5 minutes, or until browned.
3. Add the coconut milk, lime rind and juice, lime leaves and tamarind concentrate. Reduce the heat and simmer for 15 minutes, or until the chicken is cooked and the sauce has reduced and thickened slightly. Season well with salt.
4. Garnish with lime wedges and lime leaves, and serve with rice.

NUTRITION PER SERVE (6)
Protein 32 g; Fat 25 g; Carbohydrate 4 g; Dietary Fibre 1.5 g; Cholesterol 65 mg; 1590 kJ (380 cal)

Prawn salad with kaffir lime (top) and Nonya lime chicken

Flavoured oils

Using flavoured oils in your stir-fries gives a delicious boost of flavour. They are also great in salad dressings. Use good-quality vegetable oil and do not heat above 120°C (250°F) or the ingredients may burn, affecting the flavour. Sterilise jars by washing thoroughly and drying in a very slow oven (120°C/250°F/Gas 1/2) for 20 minutes.

Star anise and orange oil

Heat 300 ml oil with 75 ml good-quality peanut oil, 4 star anise and the zest of 4 large oranges in a wok to 105°C (220°F) and cook for 5 minutes. Pour into a sterilised glass jar, seal, cool and refrigerate for 2 days to infuse. Strain the solids and discard. Store in a sterilised glass jar in the fridge for up to 6 months. Makes 1 1/2 cups (375 ml)

Sesame and chilli oil

Heat 300 ml oil and 3 tablespoons chilli flakes in a wok to 105°C (220°F) and cook for 8 minutes. Remove from the heat and add 75 ml sesame oil. Strain the chillies and discard. Pour into a sterilised glass jar, seal, cool and store in the fridge for up to 6 months. Makes 1 1/2 cups (375 ml)

Ginger oil

Heat 1 1/2 cups (375 ml) oil and 400 g finely sliced fresh ginger in a wok to 105°C (220°F) and cook for 45 minutes, or until the ginger just starts to turn golden. Strain and discard the ginger. Pour into a sterilised glass jar, seal, cool and store in the fridge for up to 6 months. Makes 1 1/2 cups (375 ml)

Lime and lemon grass oil

Heat 1¹/2 cups (375 ml) oil, 2 finely chopped lemon grass stems (white part only) and the zest of 4 limes in a wok to 105°C (220°F) and cook for 5 minutes. Add 4 shredded kaffir lime leaves. Remove from the heat. Pour into a sterilised glass jar, seal, cool and refrigerate for 2 days then strain, discarding the solids. Store in a sterilised glass jar in the fridge for up to 6 months. Makes 1¹/2 cups (375 ml)

Left to right: Star anise and orange oil; Sesame and chilli oil; Ginger oil; Lime and lemon grass oil; Coriander oil; Garlic oil

Coriander oil

Blanch the leaves, stems and roots of 2 bunches (180 g) coriander in simmering water for 10 seconds. Remove and plunge into iced water. Drain well and pat dry with paper towels. Chop the coriander roughly, then process with 1¹/2 cups (375 ml) oil in a food processor. Seal in a sterilised glass jar, cool and refrigerate overnight. Strain through a fine sieve and discard any solids. Store in a sterilised glass jar in the fridge for up to 2 weeks. Makes 1¹/2 cups (375 ml)

Garlic oil

Peel one whole head of garlic, place the cloves in a bowl and cover with white vinegar or lemon juice for 24 hours. Drain, discard the vinegar and dry the garlic on paper towels. Place the garlic in a wok with 1¹/2 cups (375 ml) oil, heat to 105°C (220°F) and cook for 12 minutes, or until the garlic begins to turn golden. Pour into a sterilised glass jar, seal, cool and refrigerate overnight. Strain, discard the garlic and store in a sterilised glass jar in the fridge for up to 6 weeks. Makes 1¹/2 cups (375 ml)

Pork, pumpkin and cashew stir-fry

Preparation time:
20 minutes
Total cooking time:
20 minutes
Serves 4

2–3 tablespoons oil
1/2 cup (80 g) cashews
750 g pork neck, cut
 into long, thin strips
500 g pumpkin, cut
 into 2 cm cubes
1 tablespoon grated
 fresh ginger
1/3 cup (80 ml) chicken
 stock
1/4 cup (60 ml) dry
 sherry
1 1/2 tablespoons soy
 sauce
1/2 teaspoon cornflour
500 g baby bok choy,
 chopped
1–2 tablespoons fresh
 coriander leaves

1. Heat a wok until very hot, add 1 tablespoon oil and swirl to coat. Stir-fry the cashews for 1–2 minutes, or until browned. Drain.
2. Reheat the wok, add a little extra oil and swirl to coat. Stir-fry the pork in batches for 5 minutes, or until lightly browned. Remove. Add 1 tablespoon oil and stir-fry the pumpkin and ginger for 3 minutes, or until lightly browned. Add the stock, sherry and soy sauce, and simmer for 3 minutes, or until the pumpkin is tender.
3. Blend the cornflour with 1 teaspoon water, add to the wok and stir until the mixture boils and thickens. Return the pork and cashews to the wok, and add the bok choy and coriander. Stir until the bok choy has just wilted. Serve.

NUTRITION PER SERVE
Protein 46 g; Fat 28 g;
Carbohydrate 15 g; Dietary
Fibre 8 g; Cholesterol
75 mg; 2112 kJ (505 cal)

Eggplant with hot bean sauce

Preparation time:
20 minutes
Total cooking time:
15 minutes
Serves 4–6

1/4 cup (60 ml) peanut
 oil
800 g eggplant, cut into
 2 cm cubes
4 spring onions, chopped
3 cloves garlic, crushed
1 tablespoon finely
 chopped fresh ginger
1 tablespoon hot bean
 paste
1/2 cup (125 ml)
 vegetable stock
1/4 cup (60 ml) Chinese
 rice wine
2 tablespoons rice
 vinegar
1 tablespoon tomato
 paste
2 teaspoons soft brown
 sugar
2 tablespoons soy sauce
1 teaspoon cornflour
2 tablespoons shredded
 fresh basil

1. Heat a wok until very hot, add 1 tablespoon oil and swirl to coat. Stir-fry the eggplant in batches for 3–4 minutes, or until browned. Remove.
2. Reheat the wok, add the remaining oil and swirl to coat. Stir-fry the spring onion, garlic, ginger and bean paste for 30 seconds. Add the stock, rice wine, rice vinegar, tomato paste, sugar and soy, and stir-fry for 1 minute.
3. Blend the cornflour with 1 tablespoon water, add to the wok and bring to the boil. Return the eggplant to the wok and stir-fry for 2–3 minutes, or until cooked through. Sprinkle with basil.

NUTRITION PER SERVE (6)
Protein 2 g; Fat 10 g;
Carbohydrate 5.5 g; Dietary
Fibre 3.5 g; Cholesterol
0 mg; 550 kJ (130 cal)

Pork, pumpkin and cashew stir-fry (top)
and Eggplant with hot bean sauce

Salt and pepper squid

Preparation time:
  15 minutes +
  20 minutes marinating
Total cooking time:
  10 minutes
Serves 4

*500 g squid hoods, cut
  in half lengthways*
1/3 cup (80 ml) oil
*4 cloves garlic, finely
  chopped*
1/2 teaspoon sugar
2 teaspoons salt
*1 teaspoon ground
  black pepper*
2 tablespoons lime juice
lime wedges, to garnish

1. Rinse the squid in cold water and pat dry with paper towels. Score diagonally to form a diamond pattern. Cut into 5 x 3 cm pieces. Combine the oil, garlic, sugar, and half the salt and pepper, add the squid, toss to coat, cover and refrigerate for 20 minutes.
2. Heat a wok until very hot, add the squid in batches, and stir-fry for 1–2 minutes, or until it is just white and curls. Remove.
3. Return the squid to the wok and add the lime juice and remaining salt and pepper. Heat through. Serve with lime wedges.

NUTRITION PER SERVE
*Protein 20 g; Fat 20 g;
Carbohydrate 1.5 g; Dietary
Fibre 0.5 g; Cholesterol
250 mg; 1150 kJ (275 cal)*

Chicken chow mein with crispy noodles

Preparation time:
  20 minutes
Total cooking time:
  15 minutes
Serves 4–6

oil, for deep-frying
150 g thin egg noodles
3 cloves garlic, crushed
*3 1/2 tablespoons
  cornflour*
*2 1/2 tablespoons oyster
  sauce*
1 tablespoon soy sauce
*300 g chicken breast
  fillets, sliced*
2 tablespoons peanut oil
200 g broccoli florets
2 carrots, sliced
200 g snow peas
*425 g can straw
  mushrooms, drained*
*150 g bamboo shoots,
  sliced*
2 teaspoons sugar
*1 1/4 cups (315 ml)
  chicken stock*

1. Fill a wok one third full of oil and heat until a cube of bread dropped into the oil browns in 20 seconds. Cook the noodles in small batches for 15–20 seconds, or until they rise to the surface. Drain well.
2. Mix the garlic, 1 1/2 tablespoons cornflour, 2 teaspoons oyster sauce and 2 teaspoons soy sauce together, add the chicken and toss to coat.
3. Heat a wok until very hot, add the oil and swirl to coat. Add the chicken and stir-fry for 4–5 minutes, or until browned. Add the broccoli and carrot, and stir-fry for 1 minute. Add the snow peas, mushrooms and bamboo shoots, and stir-fry for 1 minute, or until cooked.
4. Blend the remaining oyster sauce, soy sauce and cornflour, and the sugar and stock in a bowl. Add to the wok and stir for 2 minutes, or until the sauce boils and thickens. To serve, place the noodles on a serving plate and arrange the chicken over the top.

NUTRITION PER SERVE (6)
*Protein 20 g; Fat 13 g;
Carbohydrate 30 g; Dietary
Fibre 7.5 g; Cholesterol
30 mg; 1325 kJ (317 cal)*

*Chicken chow mein with crispy noodles (top)
and Salt and pepper squid*

Stir-fried fresh rice noodles with beef

Preparation time:
10 minutes +
30 minutes marinating
Total cooking time:
15 minutes
Serves 4–6

2 cloves garlic, crushed
2 teaspoons finely
  chopped fresh ginger
1 tablespoon oyster
  sauce
2 teaspoons soy sauce
500 g sliced beef
1/4 cup (60 ml) oil
1 kg fresh rice noodles,
  sliced into 2 cm strips
100 g garlic chives,
  chopped
2 1/2 tablespoons oyster
  sauce, extra
3 teaspoons soy sauce,
  extra
1 teaspoon sugar

1. Combine the garlic, ginger, oyster and soy sauces, add the beef and toss to coat. Cover and refrigerate for 30 minutes.
2. Heat a wok until very hot, add 1 tablespoon oil and swirl to coat. Add half the beef and stir-fry for 5 minutes, or until cooked. Remove and repeat with the remaining beef. Add the remaining oil, then the noodles and stir-fry for 3–5 minutes,

or until softened.
3. Add the garlic chives, and stir-fry until just wilted. Stir in the extra oyster and soy sauces, and sugar, return the beef to the wok and toss to heat through.

NUTRITION PER SERVE (6)
*Protein 33 g; Fat 13 g;
Carbohydrate 40 g; Dietary
Fibre 1.5 g; Cholesterol
50 mg; 1295 kJ (310 cal)*

Cucumber and white fish stir-fry

Preparation time:
20 minutes
Total cooking time:
20 minutes
Serves 4

1/2 cup (60 g) plain flour
1/2 cup (60 g) cornflour
1/2 teaspoon Chinese
  five-spice
750 g firm white
  boneless fish fillets,
  such as ling, cut
  into 3 cm cubes
2 egg whites, lightly
  beaten
oil, for deep-frying
1 tablespoon oil
1 onion, cut into wedges
1 telegraph cucumber,
  halved, seeded and
  sliced diagonally
1 teaspoon cornflour,
  extra
3/4 teaspoon sesame oil

1 tablespoon soy sauce
1/3 cup (80 ml) rice
  wine vinegar
1 1/2 tablespoons soft
  brown sugar
3 teaspoons fish sauce

1. Combine the flours and five-spice, and season. Dip the fish in the egg white, drain off any excess, then toss in the flour mixture, shaking off any excess.
2. Fill a large saucepan one third full of oil and heat until a bread cube browns in 15 seconds. Cook the fish in batches for 6 minutes, or until golden brown. Drain. Keep warm.
3. Heat a wok until very hot, add 1 tablespoon oil and swirl to coat. Add the onion and stir-fry for 1 minute. Add the cucumber and stir-fry for 30 seconds.
4. Blend the cornflour with 2 tablespoons water and add to the wok with the sesame oil, soy, vinegar, sugar and fish sauce. Stir-fry for 3 minutes, or until the mixture boils and thickens. Add the fish and toss to coat. Serve.

NUTRITION PER SERVE
*Protein 43 g; Fat 16 g;
Carbohydrate 35 g; Dietary
Fibre 1 g; Cholesterol
130 mg; 1990 kJ (475 cal)*

*Stir-fried fresh rice noodles with beef (top)
and Cucumber and white fish stir-fry*

Process the fish, curry paste, sugar, fish sauce and egg until smooth.

Shape the mixture into golf ball-size balls and flatten into patties.

Thai fish cakes with cucumber salad

Preparation time:
  25 minutes
Total cooking time:
  15 minutes
Serves 6

500 g redfish fillets,
  skin removed
1¹/2 tablespoons red
  curry paste
¹/4 cup (60 g) sugar
¹/4 cup (60 ml) fish
  sauce
1 egg
200 g green beans,
  sliced
10 kaffir lime leaves,
  finely chopped
oil, for deep-frying

Cucumber salad
¹/2 cup (125 ml) white
  vinegar
¹/2 cup (125 g) sugar
¹/2 cup (125 ml) plum
  sauce
2 cloves garlic,
  crushed
2 teaspoons sambal
  oelek
¹/3 cup (80 ml) fish
  sauce
¹/2 cup (80 g) roasted
  peanuts, chopped
1 telegraph cucumber,
  halved and sliced
2 tablespoons chopped
  fresh coriander leaves

1. Process the fish in a food processor for 20 seconds. Add the curry paste, sugar, fish sauce and egg, and process for 10 seconds, or until smooth. Place in a bowl and stir in the beans and lime leaves.
2. Shape golf ball-size pieces of the mixture in wet hands, then flatten to make patties.
3. Fill a wok one third full of oil and heat until a cube of bread dropped into the oil browns in 15 seconds. Cook the fish cakes in batches for 3–5 minutes, turning to give an even colouring. Drain on paper towels and keep warm.
4. To make the salad, put the vinegar, sugar and ¹/2 cup (125 ml) water in a small saucepan, and stir over low heat until the sugar has dissolved. Add the plum sauce, garlic, sambal oelek and fish sauce, and bring to the boil, then reduce the heat and simmer for 5 minutes, or until the sauce thickens slightly. Cool. Add the remaining ingredients and mix together well. Serve with the fish cakes.

NUTRITION PER SERVE
Protein 23 g; Fat 17 g; Carbohydrate 35 g; Dietary Fibre 2.5 g; Cholesterol 90 mg; 1834 kJ (438 cal)

Thai fish cakes with cucumber salad

Cook the fish cakes in batches, then drain on paper towels.

Add the peanuts, coriander and cucumber to the sauce and mix well.

61

Stir-fried fish with ginger

Preparation time:
20 minutes
Total cooking time:
15 minutes
Serves 4

1 tablespoon peanut oil
1 small onion, finely
  sliced
3 teaspoons ground
  coriander
600 g boneless white
  fish fillets, such as
  perch, cut into bite-
  size strips
1 tablespoon julienned
  fresh ginger
1 teaspoon finely
  chopped and seeded
  green chilli
2 tablespoons lime juice
2 tablespoons fresh
  coriander leaves

1. Heat a wok until very
hot, add the oil and
swirl to coat. Add the
onion and stir-fry for
4 minutes, or until soft
and golden. Add the
ground coriander and
cook for 1–2 minutes,
or until fragrant.
2. Add the fish, ginger
and chilli, and stir-fry
for 5–7 minutes, or
until the fish is cooked
through. Stir in the
lime juice and season.
Garnish with the
coriander leaves and
serve with boiled rice.

NUTRITION PER SERVE
*Protein 30 g; Fat 9 g;
Carbohydrate 1 g; Dietary
Fibre 0.4 g; Cholesterol
105 mg; 895 kJ (214 cal)*

Warm lamb salad

Preparation time:
15 minutes +
3 hours refrigeration
Total cooking time:
15 minutes
Serves 4–6

2 tablespoons red curry
  paste
1/4 cup (15 g) chopped
  fresh coriander leaves
1 tablespoon finely
  grated fresh ginger
3–4 tablespoons peanut
  oil
750 g lamb fillets,
  thinly sliced
200 g snow peas
600 g packet thick
  fresh rice noodles
1 red capsicum, thinly
  sliced
1 Lebanese cucumber,
  thinly sliced
6 spring onions, thinly
  sliced

Mint dressing
1 1/2 tablespoons
  peanut oil
1/4 cup (60 ml) lime
  juice
2 tablespoons soft
  brown sugar
3 teaspoons fish sauce

3 teaspoons soy sauce
1/3 cup (20 g) chopped
  fresh mint leaves
1 clove garlic, crushed

1. Combine the curry
paste, coriander, ginger
and 2 tablespoons oil
in a bowl. Add the
lamb and coat well.
Cover and refrigerate
for 2–3 hours.
2. Steam or boil the
snow peas until just
tender, refresh under
cold water and drain.
3. Cover the noodles
with boiling water.
Leave for 5 minutes, or
until tender, and drain.
4. To make the dressing,
put all the ingredients
in a jar and shake well.
5. Heat a wok until very
hot, add 1 tablespoon
oil and swirl to coat.
Add half the lamb and
stir-fry for 5 minutes,
or until tender. Repeat
with the remaining
lamb, using more oil
if needed.
6. Place the lamb,
snow peas, noodles,
capsicum, cucumber
and spring onion in a
large bowl, drizzle with
the dressing and toss to
combine. Serve.

NUTRITION PER SERVE (6)
*Protein 32 g; Fat 20 g;
Carbohydrate 33 g; Dietary
Fibre 3 g; Cholesterol
83 mg; 1850 kJ (442 cal)*

*Stir-fried fish with ginger (top)
and Warm lamb salad*

Index